Aftertaste

Ciara Elizabeth Smyth

T0353525

methuen | drama

LONDON • NEW YORK • OXFORD • NEW DELHI • SYDNEY

METHUEN DRAMA
Bloomsbury Publishing Plc
50 Bedford Square, London, WC1B 3DP, UK
1385 Broadway, New York, NY 10018, USA
29 Earlsfort Terrace, Dublin 2, Ireland

BLOOMSBURY, METHUEN DRAMA and the Methuen
Drama logo are trademarks of Bloomsbury Publishing Plc

First published in Great Britain 2021

A catalogue record for this book is available from the British Library.

A catalog record for this book is available from the Library of Congress.

ISBN: PB: 978-1-3502-8777-8
ePDF: 978-1-3502-8778-5
eBook: 978-1-3502-8779-2

Series: Modern Plays

Typeset by Mark Heslington Ltd, Scarborough, North Yorkshire

To find out more about our authors and books visit
www.bloomsbury.com and sign up for our newsletters.

YOUTH THEATRE IRELAND

National Youth Theatre 2021
in association with the Abbey Theatre

Aftertaste by Ciara Elizabeth Smyth

Commissioned by Youth Theatre Ireland for the National Youth
Theatre 2021

Creative Team:

Artistic Director	Veronica Coburn
Dramaturg	Lakesha Arie-Angelo
Producer	Kelly Phelan
Producer for Youth Theatre Ireland	Eoghan Doyle
Composer/Sound Design	Sinéad Diskin
Lighting Designer	Suzi Cummins
Visual/Costume Design	Cherie White
Production Manager	Éanna Whelan
Stage Manager	Clive Welsh
ASM	Meabh Crowe
Hair and Make-Up	Sarah Naylor
Head of Welfare	Louise Holian
Welfare Support	Cathal Thornton
Welfare Support	Gary Mullen
Producing Intern	Katerina Mullalli

Performance Ensemble

Abbi Breen
Aileen Briody
Matthew Eglinton
Odhran Exton
Samuel Ferrie
Abhainn Harrington
Daisy Hartigan
Adam Henry
Seán Loughrey
Sadhbh McDonough
Cara Mooney
Max Mufwasoni
Ella O'Callaghan
Caoimhe O'Farrell
Tristan Spellman Molphy
Julia Szarota

Design Ensemble

Lara Coady
Emma Corrigan
Ellen Donohue
William McCabe
Aoibhinn McGinley
Feargal Quinn

Aftertaste

For the cast

Characters

THE ROYAL MARINE STAFF

Aidan Proctor	**Head Chef**	Abhainn Harrington
Mason Mbayo	**Sous Chef**	Max Mufwasoni
Cora Greene	**Chef de Partie**	Cara Mooney
Eadie Birch	**Pâtissier**	Ella O'Callaghan
Anthony Glover	**Kitchen Porter**	Adam Henry
Anastasia O'Kane	**Restaurant Manager**	Aileen Briody
Stephen McLoughlin	**Waiter**	Seán Loughrey

OUTSIDE EYES

Margot Murphy	**Actor**	Sadhbh McDonough
Lila Birch	**Junk Advocate**	Daisy Hartigan
Oisín Ó Hanluain	**News Reporter**	Odhran Exton

NATIONAL ALLIANCE PARTY

Sanbrooke Martin	**President**	Samuel Ferrie
Jana Kaminski	**Vice President**	Julia Szarota
Ty Costello	**Chief of Staff**	Tristan Spellman Molphy
Malachi Kelly	**Head of Security**	Matthew Eglinton
Cordelia Flowers	**Press Secretary**	Caoimhe O'Farrell
Ava Poppler	**Civil Servant**	Abbi Breen

OTHER CHARACTERS

Director	**Guard One**
VO	**Guard Two**

Additional characters can be played or voiced by any members of the cast.

Notes on the text

CW

Sex, food, drink, racism, torture, murder and violent imagery.

Setting

A world of young politicians and a seemingly left-leaning government.

The Health and Wellness Act, passed one year before the events of this play, has made it illegal to possess or consume unhealthy food or 'junk'.

All fast-food chains have been expelled from the country and the government is pushing the nation towards an unprocessed, plant-based diet. There has been a rising number of 'Junk Advocates', a term coined for people who actively and openly acquire and consume illegal foods and encourage others to do so.

Any character's gender/pronouns can be changed as the director sees fit.

This play is based on and inspired by material from workshops with the cast.

'Behold, The Devil is about to throw some of you in prison'

Chapter One: The Missing Girl

One: Utopia

Eadie's *eyes.*

A major channel news report in the field.

CAPTION: 'Oisín Ó Hanluain for TDT News'.

Oisín   Good evening. Today marks the one-year anniversary of the government's contentious Health and Wellness Act, borne from a nationwide desire to aid herd immunity. The Act mandates that the possession and consumption of addictive foods, such as those with a high sugar or fat content, is illegal. As the price of fresh food rises and the nation's hunger grows, the Government is coming under increasing pressure from 'Junk Advocates' to repeal the act. Some politicians have even called for the resignation of President Sandbrooke Martin, who remains unrepentant and defiant.

Eadie's *eyes.*

A ringing in her ears.

CUT TO: A video on social media.

Lila, *indoors and smiling. The light is amazing.*

CAPTION: 'What I eat in a day as a person who eats whatever the fugg they want'.

Lila   What I eat in a day as a person who eats whatever the fuck they want.

The following text is heard as food is presented either in person or in video clips.

Lila   For breakfast I used a large bar of Dairy Milk as a spoon to eat Nutella. For second breakfast I had a crisp sandwich (*CAPTION: 'salt and vinegar + cheese and onion'*) because I'm a fucking genius. Lunch was a plate of triple-

cooked chips and French toast with maple syrup. Pre-dinner
snack was a plate of crackers with sugar and butter. Dinner
was caramelised bacon pasta with garlic bread and dessert
was chocolate-covered strawberries because HEALTH.
Almost all illegal commodities now but I so deeply don't give
a fuck about what the Government wants me to eat, it's
palpable. And where did I get this unholy mess of brown
and beige? You can get anything online if you look
hard enough.

Eadie*'s eyes welling up.*

Blackout.

Eadie   My sister has been missing for six days.

*We hear the thump of heavy bass and an uncomfortable, menacing
drone. The beat starts to speed up.*

*We see each character for a split second, alone in front of a mirror as
they prepare.*

Aidan Proctor *is combing his hair and checking for bald spots.*

Mason Mbayo *is meditating and repeating affirmations in the
mirror ('Tu peux le faire – Tu peux le faire – Tu peux le faire'
meaning 'You can do it') .*

Anastasia O'Kane *is applying makeup slowly and purposefully.*

Sanbrooke Martin *is having a suit fitted and scrolling angrily
through his phone.*

Cordelia Flowers *is practising laughs and agreeing with people.*

Ty Costello *is polishing his shoes and bringing them into the light
to inspect them, something is shining in his mouth – a diamond tooth.*

Stephen McLoughlin *is doing power poses and listening to
heavy metal.*

Cora Greene *is cleaning a sex toy – when she's done she looks in
the mirror and ruffles her eyebrows.*

Jana Kaminski *is having her hair done (in foils) and smoking.*

Margot Murphy *is taking pills and doing vocal warm-ups.*

Anthony Glover *is scrubbing a stain out of a top, when he's done he finds another stain and starts scrubbing that.*

Malachi Kelly *is trying on eyepatches, but decides in the end to go without.*

Oisín Ó Hanluain *is holding a bottle of hairspray and practising his acceptance speech for Journalist of the Year, an award he has never been nominated for.*

Ava Poppler *is trying on blazers with matching clipboards and biting her nails.*

Eadie Birch *is not looking in the mirror but out a window, watching two pigeons have sex. She looks towards the mirror when her phone rings. She answers it.*

Lila Birch *is not at her bathroom mirror but the tap is left running. There is a shopping bag with spilled milk and cracked eggs on the floor.*

Silence.

Eadie   My sister has been missing for six days. And I think you know where she is.

Music starts again.

*A line of torches and crowds of people calling **Lila**'s name.*

*A poster with the title 'HAVE YOU SEEN MY SISTER?' over a picture of **Lila**.*

*A clip of an interview with actor **Margot Murphy** on a red carpet.*

CAPTION: 'Actor – Margot Murphy'.

Margot   I don't live there anymore, but the Government has a lot to answer for, I mean food prices are skyrocketing, people are starving, rations are inadequate. It's a crisis. Those who have the least are – (*She's touched on the shoulder by someone.*) Oh hi. (*Back to the microphone.*) They're paying for the actions of those who have the most, you know? And people are going missing, that girl. It's just. Awful.

A homemade video of **Lila** *flipping pancakes at home and laughing with another girl whose face has been blurred.*

Major channel news report, **Oisín** *is still in the field, perhaps in a different location.*

Oisín   As the tide of public opinion continues to turn against the Health and Wellness Act, police are still appealing for any information on the disappearance of twenty-one-year-old Lila Birch, a Junk Advocate, who was last seen outside her Dublin city centre apartment six days ago. In a press conference this morning, President and leader of the National Alliance Party, Sanbrooke Martin, and the Vice President, Jana Kaminski, called for the search for Lila to be widened. This reporter was on the scene.

Two: Tits 'N' Teeth

A few dozen reporters at a press conference.

Press Secretary **Cordelia Flowers** *is at the podium.*

Civil Servant **Ava Poppler** *stands somewhere off camera, clutching a clipboard.*

All National Alliance Party members and affiliates are dressed in various shades of pink.

Cordelia   Thank you for coming, this will be very brief, the President and the Vice President are pushed for time today. Before they join us I'd like to remind everyone for the love of God please keep the questions on topic, OK? Nothing on the recent smear campaign against the President. I will shut this down if I hear one word about the tortoise photo or the alleged love child or the misuse of campaign funds. (*Correcting herself.*) Alleged misuse, alleged. And please be respectful. Ps and Qs people. That means you, Oisín.

Oisín   Have you seen this morning's polls, Cordelia? The President's approval rating is down seven points.

Cordelia   I will ask you to leave Oisín. Do you want me to do that? Keep a lid on it. (*Addressing the crowd.*) Right, we'll finish up just before 2pm. Preliminary questions? No? Good. (*Under her breath.*) Christ.

Cordelia *steps aside and starts typing furiously on her phone.*

A door opens at the side and in walks President **Sanbrooke Martin** *and Vice President* **Jana Kaminski**.

A cacophony of clicking cameras.

Sanbrooke   Good afternoon. I'm sorry we have to be here at all. I would like to begin by paying tribute to Lila Birch's family, for their fortitude and forbearance, for what could only be the most intensely difficult week of their lives. Lila has now been missing six days. The police have failed to make any progress. Let me say that again, the police have failed. And it is unacceptable. I know it is, you know it is. God knows what they're doing. So –

We are calling for the search for Lila to be expanded. We implore the public, if you have any information regarding the disappearance of Lila or know anything about her whereabouts, please come forward. Our goal is to find Lila safe and sound. And for Lila's family to put this horrific time behind them. Cordelia.

Press Secretary **Cordelia Flowers** *steps forward.*

Cordelia   We're happy to field one or two questions at this point.

Reporters stick their hands up.

Oisín   Has anyone been in touch with the Birch family?

Jana (*stepping forward*)   Yes. Of course we have been in touch with the Birch family. And we will continue to be in close communication with them.

Oisín   Do you think Lila was targeted?

Jana   The police seem to think it was a planned abduction, yes.

Sanbrooke *looks slightly irritated that* **Jana** *keeps answering the questions.*

Sanbrooke   I think we give someone else a go / now

Oisín   Sorry Mr President, just one more, Lila Birch openly spoke out against your Health and Wellness Act, she consistently posted videos of herself with banned food and encouraged her large following to do the same so /

Cordelia   I feel like you've had enough ques/tions

Oisín   Does the President think her Junk Advocacy had anything to do with her disappearance?

Pause.

Sanbrooke   We're appealing for information over a missing woman here.

Oisín   Yes but / what

Jana   In short, no. We do not believe her Junk Advocacy had anything to do with her disappearance. While The Health and Wellness Act does make certain addictive processed foods illegal, the penalty is minor. It was never our intention to ban foods but rather to shift the focus to fuelling bodies correctly for herd immunity. The foods eliminated have been scientifically linked to heart disease, cancer, eating disorders, obesity, hyperactivity, anxiety, I mean, you name it. Instead of begging the country to make the healthy choice, our party has removed the option of junk. Of course, as with any illegal substance there are methods and means of acquiring them, and yes Lila did spend time acquiring junk but her punishment would have been a fine. About €100 I think. It's not a serious crime. We have absolutely no reason to believe that Lila's disappearance had anything to do with her online persona.

Oisín   Lila was causing the Government a lot of trouble. She was gaining a massive following flouting your policies.

Sanbrooke   What are you suggesting?

Oisín   I'm suggesting your Government benefits from her disappearance.

Sanbrooke   That is vile, vile conjecture, no proof.

Oisín   That's not entirely true, I have information that suggests government involvement in the leak of Lila Birch's address.

Beat.

A flurry of reporters standing up to ask questions.

Cordelia   You know what, I think that's all the questions we'll take for today. Thank you.

Cordelia *shoots* **Oisín** *a filthy look.*

End of press conference. **Sanbrooke** *glares at* **Oisín** *then he and* **Jana** *leave, quickly followed by* **Cordelia** *and* **Ava**.

Cordelia   Sorry. I'm so sorry about him.

Sanbrooke   Every time, every single time, you let him talk as if he's the only reporter there. Ava, revoke his press pass.

Ava   Okey-dokey.

Cordelia   I'm sorry, I'm so sorry he won't be here again.

Sanbrooke   He won't be here again, because I'm banning him.

Ava   Do you want me to give a reason for revoking his press pass?

Sanbrooke   Yes. You can tell him it was revoked because he is a cunt.

Ava *has a notepad and pen in her hand and starts writing that down.*

Ava (*whispers*)   Cunt.

Jana   Don't write that down.

Ava   Okey-dokey.

Scribbles out 'Cunt'.

Sanbrooke   Pass it along verbally, Ava. Where is he getting his information about the address leak? That's not a rhetorical question, Cordelia, I want an answer. Jesus Christ, controlling the press is literally your only job.

Cordelia   I know, I do know that. I don't know where he's getting his information from.

Sanbrooke   Well find out.

Cordelia (*nodding*)   No. Of course. Yes.

Sanbrooke   I mean who actually cares about that loud mouth little bitch Lila Birch? Stuffing crisps into her face, that's what she was famous for, good fucking riddance.

Jana *looks shocked.*

Ava *and* **Cordelia** *look away.*

Sanbrooke   Don't give me that look, Jana, you were thinking it. Cordelia, from where I'm standing, you are surplus to requirement, do you know what that means?

Cordelia   Does it mean like, that you don't need me?

Sanbrooke   Yes it does. One more mistake, just one and you're done. Get out of my sight.

Cordelia *nods and exits down the hallway in the opposite direction.*

Sanbrooke   He actually accused us of kidnapping people.

Jana   I know.

Sanbrooke   Ava, call my tailor, tell her I've changed my mind, I want the bubble gum. Magenta is bullshit, she was right. But don't tell her she was right.

Ava (*writing*)   Tailor, bubble gum, not right. Got it.

Jana   And Ava, get in touch with the Birch family.

Ava   Have we not been in touch?

Sanbrooke   Have we not been in touch with the
Birch family?

Jana   Well I haven't. Have you?

Sanbrooke   No.

Jana (*kindly*)   Of course you haven't. When would we have
the time? We're spinning plates here. Ava, you do it. You
already know the address.

Ava *stops writing for a split second, mortified.*

Sanbrooke   Ava, also, cancel my 4pm appearance at the
soup kitchen, I don't want to deal with those clamouring
skeletons telling me they're hungry.

Jana   Ava, I'll go to that.

Sanbrooke   As well I've changed my mind about the dinner.
I want a small affair, speak to Costello, tell him to cancel the
banquet, banquets are gauche. They're bullshit. Ask him to
find a new restaurant. Just the five. Are you getting
this down?

They reach the end of the corridor.

Ava (*writing*)   Yes, yes. Cancel banquet. Five guests /

Sanbrooke   Can I ask you a genuine question. Are
you stupid?

Ava (*brief pause*)   I don't . . . I mean I don't know what
barometer . . . no.

Sanbrooke   Then stop repeating everything I'm saying.
(*Muttering.*) Completely incompetent. (*Loudly.*) Just, look.
Tell Costello I want a new venue. Something small. And
check the status of our special guest. Go.

Ava *rushes off.*

Sanbrooke *and* **Jana** *face each other.*

Sanbrooke   How do I look?

Jana   Thin.

Sanbrooke   Good.

They exchange forced smiles and turn to enter rooms opposite each other.

Three: White Torture

Margot *is sitting on a chair in an all-white room. She has a white bag over her head and her hands are tied in front of her. There are white security cameras on the ceiling in the corners of the room. Everything in the room is white, including the costumes of those who enter.*

Margot *has the dressed-down style of a young Frances McDormand. She is wearing flat shoes, muted colours and practical clothes. Chief of Staff* **Mr Costello** *and Head of Security* **Mr Kelly** *enter.* **Mr Costello** *is drinking a tumbler of frozen vodka. They are disarmingly jolly.*

Mr Kelly   I didn't go with it in the end.

Mr Costello   You thought it was too much?

Mr Kelly   It felt like too much.

Mr Costello   Like a cartoon villain, sort of?

Mr Kelly   A bit like a cartoon villain yeah.

Mr Costello   That's a pity. You were so excited about it.

Mr Kelly   Well listen, never say never.

Mr Costello   Sure. Yeah. (*Pointing at* **Margot**.) Do you see who's here?

Mr Kelly   I'm so excited.

Mr Costello   Shall we?

They count silently one, two, three.

Mr Kelly (*taking the bag off her head*)   Ms Murphy!

Mr Costello   I loved you in *Midnight Forever*.

Mr Kelly   That's my favourite film.

Mr Costello   You're my favourite actor.

Mr Kelly   We can't believe you're here.

Margot   What is this?

Mr Costello   The best day of my life.

Mr Kelly   Do you know who we are?

Margot *looks at them.*

Margot   No.

Mr Kelly   And sure, why would you.

Mr Costello   We're with The National Alliance Party and we're big fans.

Mr Kelly   Huge. We can quote all your films.

Mr Costello (*quoting her movies*)   'Somebody shot Timmy!'

Mr Kelly   'Who let *you* back in Glenbrook Manor?'

Mr Costello   'Madam President. It's your husband. He's dead.'

Mr Kelly   'I can't love you, Éamon de Valera, I can't.'

Margot   They're all from the same film.

Mr Costello   *Midnight Forever.* My favourite.

Mr Kelly   The President's favourite too.

Mr Costello   He still talks about the shoes you wore.

Mr Kelly   Those shoes.

Mr Costello   I think he really relates to your character. And how she can't love Éamon de Valera.

Margot   The President knows you kidnapped me?

Mr Costello   I don't think we said that.

Margot   Look. Can you untie me?

Mr Kelly   I don't see why not, you're not going anywhere.

Mr Kelly *cuts the cable ties from her wrists with a hunting knife, which is also white. He then returns it to its sheath on his belt.*

Margot   Thank you. (*Beat.*) I need my inhaler.

Mr Kelly   We didn't find any / inhal

Margot   It was in my bag. It's there. Just look, please.

Mr Costello *looks through her bag and passes her the inhaler. She shakes it and breathes deeply.*

Margot   Now. Why am I here?

Mr Kelly   Well before we get into that /

Margot   No, I'd like to get into that now. Last thing I remember was attending the Olivier nominees luncheon and now I'm here. It is possible that I had one too many Moets but I think it's more likely that you had me drugged and kidnapped. Am I right?

Mr Kelly   You're very astute.

Mr Costello   We didn't *not* have you drugged.

Margot   Why am I here?

Mr Costello   Did Karl not explain?

Margot   Who's Karl?

Mr Kelly   He was your driver. Well Karl's not his real name.

Mr Costello   But he should have explained.

Margot   He didn't explain.

Mr Kelly   I can't believe Karl didn't explain. He's our best guy.

Margot   As much as I am enjoying this double act, I need a straight answer.

Mr Costello   Absolutely. So. You're going to a dinner party.

Mr Kelly   A dinner party. With the President.

Margot   A dinner party with the President?

Mr Costello   You'll be the guest of honour.

Mr Kelly   Exciting.

Margot   Is that it?

Mr Kelly   There is something else.

Mr Costello   You caught us.

Mr Kelly   She's sharp.

Mr Costello   Before the festivities, I would like you to do a quick interview with the press.

Mr Kelly   A five-minute news thing.

Margot   What do you want me to say?

Mr Costello   I think we'd like you to take back some comments you made earlier in the week.

Mr Kelly   'The Government has a lot to answer for'?

Mr Costello   Yuck.

Mr Kelly   You're very popular, and that made us look bad. So we'd like you to take it back.

Mr Costello   The President would like you to take it back.

Margot   You brought me here for a comment I made?

Mr Kelly   Yes. You can't just go around saying whatever you want.

Margot   I think you'll find I can.

Mr Costello   I think you'll find you can't. We can't just let people say whatever they like. You only have to open a history book to see the damage that is caused when people say and do whatever they like.

Margot   Look, I don't even remember what I said, I'm not politically motivated, that talk just plays well on the red carpet. I don't care what you're doing, I made a comment. Actions and words are not the same thing.

Mr Costello   Words have repercussions. Do you think it would be right for me to allow people to advocate misogyny? Would it be right to let people spread racist views and encourage violence? Is it right for people to use their voices to incite hatred?

Margot   That is not what I was doing.

Mr Costello   You were spreading false information about the Government. You also implied /

Mr Kelly   Heavily implied /

Mr Costello   Heavily implied, that government legislation had something to do with the disappearance of a young woman. It was disgusting. Your words have consequences. And we're here to show you that.

There is a knock on the door and it opens to reveal **Ava**.

Ava   Mr Costello?

Mr Costello   Get out.

Ava *hurriedly closes the door.*

Margot   Help!

Mr Kelly   Please. She works for us.

Margot   What if I refuse to do the press conference?

Mr Kelly   Why would you refuse?

Mr Costello   Are you refusing?

Margot   What happens if I refuse?

Mr Costello   We don't like hypotheticals. So we'll just leave you here to have a think about our little proposal.

A door opens, apparently on its own, and the men walk out.

Mr Kelly   That went well.

Mr Costello   Absolutely it did.

The door closes and then a flap in the door opens and a white gloved hand passes through a plate of unseasoned white rice with a white spoon.

Four: Dungeons

Later that day, **Ava** *is in* **Cordelia Flowers'** *office.*

Cordelia   Ava I've had a compliment about you. No sorry, not a compliment, a complaint. You understand you work for the Civil Service, yes? That's not too difficult for you to comprehend? You can't just go walking around government buildings willy nilly. Think, Ava. Use your noodle. Yeah? Mr Costello is livid.

I mean what's your clearance level?

Ava   Seven.

Cordelia   Jesus Christ. Seven? What were you even doing in that part of the building?

Ava   The President had an urgent request for Mr Costello, I was trying to find him.

Cordelia   Bullshit. You could have called him.

Ava   He wasn't answering.

Cordelia   No one believes that's why you were there. I'm not going to lie to you, the President knows about this. The smear campaign has him on edge, he thinks someone is out to get him. So you wandering around a restricted area to supposedly pass on dinner plans, is suspicious, it just is. Look Ava. I'm your friend. I want to be on your side. You need to tell me the truth.

Ava   That is the truth, I was looking for Mr Costello.

Beat.

Cordelia   Did you agree with what the President said about Lila Birch?

Ava   I can't remember what he said.

Cordelia   He called her a loud mouth little bitch. Do you agree with that?

Ava *shrugs.*

Cordelia   Do you agree with Junk Advocates?

Ava (*pause*)   No.

Cordelia   Where do you think Oisín got his information that the government was involved in the leak of Lila's address?

Ava   I have no idea.

Cordelia   Two weeks ago you filed a detailed report on Lila Birch. That report included her address.

Ava   I didn't /

Cordelia   Have you been talking to Oisín, Ava?

Ava   No.

Cordelia   Is that what you were doing? Snooping around to give Oisín more information?

Ava   I didn't give him anything.

Cordelia   Then maybe you put Lila's address online.

Ava   I would never do that.

Cordelia   Oh I believe you, but you can see how it looks.

Ava   How does it look?

Mr Costello *walks through the open door.* **Ava** *gets a fright.*

Mr Costello   Ava.

Ava   Mr Costello. I'm so sorry for walking in on you like that.

Mr Costello   Are you?

Ava   Yes.

Beat.

Ava   The President has an urgent request for you to find a new venue for dinner. Just five guests.

Mr Costello   Does he? Well tell you what, since you're so eager today, why don't you sort that out?

Ava *doesn't respond.*

Mr Costello   Did you need something else?

Ava   No.

Cordelia   Ava one more mistake, just one and you're fired.

Ava *leaves.* **Cordelia** *looks at* **Mr Costello***'s glass.*

Cordelia   Is that vodka?

Mr Costello   She needs to be reprimanded.

Cordelia   So it's not vodka?

Mr Costello   Did you hear what I said?

Cordelia   I was reprimanding her.

Mr Costello   Well next time I'll do it.

Five: Blood Of The Lamb

Eadie's *eyes.*

A ringing sound.

CUT TO: A video on social media.

Lila, *indoors and smiling. The light, again, is amazing.*

Comment on screen: 'f@t fukcin bithc that's over 3000 calories, stop promoting obesity'.

Lila (*V/O*)   OK I want to address this comment. I usually get these when people only bother to look at one of my food videos and they don't know what I look like. I obviously benefit from thin privilege, I have a really high metabolism, I actually find it difficult to put on weight. Still I think this kind of comment is absurd and honestly, violent, in this day and age. The purpose of a comment like this is to make the person it's directed at hate themselves. And I know that impetus to inflict pain on something, comes from being in serious pain yourself, so I'm sorry for your pain, author of this comment. But also from the bottom of my heart, suck my fucking tits.

Eadie's *eyes.*

Doorbell.

Ava *and* **Eadie** *sit across from each other. They each have a cup and saucer and there is a plate of biscuits between them.*

Ava (*gesturing to the plate*)   Are these / real?

Eadie   There's no sugar.

Ava *takes one and bites into it.*

Ava   I wasn't asking, it's – That's really good. What's in them?

Eadie   Banana and peanut butter.

Ava   That's the nicest thing I've had in ages.

Eadie   I'm a pâtissier. Well, I was.

Ava   Right.

Eadie   I still work in a kitchen, but not with sugar anymore. Obviously.

Ava   Where do you work?

Eadie   The Royal Marine.

Ava   That's nice.

Brief pause.

Ava   I don't really know what I'm doing here.

Eadie   Have you been sent to console me?

Ava   I'm not consoling you though.

Eadie   No you're not.

Ava (*pause*)   I'm sorry about your sister.

Eadie *nods.*

Eadie   Everyone keeps saying that. Is there any new information?

Ava   No.

Eadie   Nothing? Have her cards been used, has anyone seen her? Is there nothing at all?

Ava   I'm just a civil servant, I don't have that information.

Eadie   Then why are you here?

Ava   I was asked to get in touch with the family. I couldn't find anything for your parents, are they /

Eadie   They're not with us anymore.

Ava   Oh.

Eadie   Why are you here?

Ava   I don't know.

Pause.

Ava   Can I have another biscuit?

Eadie   Six days.

Ava   Sorry?

Eadie   My sister has been missing for six days. And no one knows anything.

Eadie*'s eyes.*

Eadie   I can't stop checking my phone.

Ava*'s eyes.*

Eadie   I can't think.

Ava   I have to tell you something.

Eadie   What?

Ava   Something the President said about your sister.

Blackout.

Beat.

CUT TO: A major channel news report.

Oisín   The body of a young woman has been found in the Grand Canal this evening. Police believe it to be the body of Lila Birch and a laceration on her neck is suspected to be the cause of death.

Ava*'s eyes.*

Chapter Two: The Rat

Six: Purple Sprouting Broccoli

The National Alliance Health and Wellness Campaign commercial shot thirteen months ago.

The focus is heavily on glamour shots of the President **Sanbrooke Martin** *and the Vice President* **Jana Kaminski***, holding cucumbers, laughing with mandarins and waving purple sprouting broccoli. Cut with shots of groups of women holding salads, people playing tennis, fields full of vegetables and the sea.*

Sanbrooke *(V/O)*   Exhausted. Lethargic. Unfocussed. These are complaints from the healthiest among us after lockdown.

Jana *(V/O)*   Weight loss, appetite control and reduced risk of disease. Now doesn't that sound fun?

Sanbrooke   The Health and Wellness Act is our way of ensuring your future.

Jana   A plant-based diet may reduce the risk of coronary heart disease by 40 per cent and the risk of developing metabolic syndrome and type 2 diabetes by half.

Sanbrooke   We all obviously want to look good!

Jana   And while looking good is not our primary objective /

Sanbrooke   It almost is!

Jana *(smiling)*   Almost. But there are many other benefits of the Health and Wellness Act.

Sanbrooke   The Health and Wellness Act will ensure the country eats only the best of the best. Because you are what you eat. And Ireland is the best.

It's clear **Jana** *hated that sentence but she tries to cover it.*

V/O   This message has been approved by President Sanbrooke Martin and the National Alliance. The following foods are now banned.

A rapid list of foods flies up the screen as credits.

Blackout.

A soundstage shooting the commercial.

Director   And cut.

Sanbrooke (*throws a cucumber across the room*)   Get this thing away from me.

Jana   Thank you, Gerald.

Director   No problem, Ms Vice President.

Sanbrooke   Jana, if I can be honest for just one second?

Jana (*to the* **Director**)   How's Margaret?

Director   Oh she's well thank you for asking.

Jana (*to the* **Director**)   Great.

Sanbrooke   Jana? Can I be honest for a second?

Jana   Of course.

Sanbrooke   That wasn't . . . good. I know you won't mind me saying but you have very little charisma. Zero, in fact.

Jana (*sweetly*)   Really? Well thank you sir. I will take that into consideration.

Sanbrooke (*to the* **Director**)   Gerald, shall we go for another one? Because of Jana? The way her face was.

Jana   Gerald can I just take five? Thank you darling.

Jana *walks with great energy to a dressing room.*

Mr Costello *follows her in.*

Jana (*coolly*)   I have no charisma?

Mr Costello   Is that what he said?

Jana   Me. I have no charisma.

Mr Costello   He has no tact, Jana.

Jana   He has no brains, Ty. I am oozing charisma. It's coming out of my pores. Look! You can see it. And he can see it. I don't know how much longer I can do this, I don't know how much longer I can sit there and listen to his drivel. Did you hear yesterday he flat out told a journalist about the immigration stats fiasco?

Mr Costello   I did.

Jana   He just told him. He's a liability, Ty.

Mr Costello   All of the research indicates his popularity has been on a steady incline /

Jana   Fuck the research.

Mr Costello   Jana there's no getting around it, the country loves him. More and more with each passing day, his numbers have never been higher.

Jana   And how long do you think that's going to last when this Health and Wellness Act comes into effect? He's banning sugar. He's banning food.

Mr Costello   Technically the party is banning /

Jana   No no. No no, he is. He pushed this through. That's his legacy. Do you honestly think his numbers will hold when the country sees how drastic this is? This Act deprives the country not only of food but of choice. And make no mistake sooner or later the country will buck. (*Smiling.*) This is catastrophic.

Mr Costello   The party is confident /

Jana   Well I am not confident. I'm his Vice, I couldn't come out and say it but mark my words now this Act will be our ruin if we don't do something.

Beat.

Jana   He's a sinking ship and you know it.

Mr Costello   So what do you propose?

Beat.

Jana   Let's help him sink.

Mr Costello   How?

Jana   Humiliation, ruin and removal.

Seven: On Your Marks

The Royal Marine; A professional kitchen – empty.

There are two doors, one either side of the stage leading into the dining room and one at the back of the stage leading to a stairway, past which are the stores and a walk-in freezer. Past the freezer there is a connecting corridor to the dining room. In the basement are the locker rooms, bathrooms, breakroom and wine cellar.

The **Pâtissier***'s section should be nearest to the audience.*

Cora *(Chef de Partie) enters from the door at the back and* **Anna** *(Restaurant Manager) enters from the dining room. They pause for a moment when they see each other, then they busy themselves.*

Cora   Hey.

Anna   Hi.

Cora   You're in early.

Anna   As are you.

Cora   Did he call you in?

Anna   He did. I was making chips in the oven at the time.

Cora *(pretending to be scandalised)*   Were you?

Anna   Yeah, I thought it was the police on the phone.

Cora   I hope you didn't tell Aidan about the chips, he'll rat on you.

Anna   You don't tell him either.

Cora   I might.

Anna   You won't.

Cora   Why not? I think I'd make a good rat.

Anna   But you won't rat on me, because you fancy me.

Brief pause.

Cora (*smiling*)   Do I?

Anna (*smiling*)   You do.

Aidan (*Head Chef*) *walks in through the back door with a phone to his ear and about ten pieces of paper in his hand.*

Aidan (*to* **Anna**)   What are you doing in here?

Anna   Oh hello Aidan, lovely to see you too. You called me in.

Aidan   Anna I'm not wasting time on pleasantries.

Anna   Why would you?

Aidan (*pointing towards the dining room*)   Is Stephen in there?

Anna   Not yet.

Aidan   Right yeah. (*Into the phone.*) Fifteen minutes. (*To* **Cora**.) Cora, will you give me a shout when everyone's in. Anna, don't be distracting my staff.

Aidan *goes into the dining room.*

Anna   He's so much fun.

Cora   Oh my god so much fun.

Anna   Just so carefree, you know?

Cora   Not a care in the world. Do you know yesterday he took me aside and very gently told me that I should shove my job up inside my hole if I couldn't cook an artichoke.

Anna   It's good advice.

Cora   I thought so. (*Looking towards the dining room.*) He's particularly brisk today, he must actually have something to do.

Anna   He told me on the phone we're booked out tonight.

Cora   We're not?

Anna   The whole place.

Cora   Good for us. We haven't been booked out in a year, I can't believe the doors are still open.

Anna   I know. (*Brief pause.*) Are you doing anything after work?

Cora   Dunno.

Beat.

Anna   So c'mere, when were you going to ask me out?

Cora (*amused*)   Sorry?

Anna   You heard me.

Cora   I don't usually go out with people I work with.

Anna   Yeah but you work in the kitchen and I work in the dining room so really we're working beside each other. Adjacent, like.

Cora   That's splitting hairs. Have you ever gone out with a colleague?

Anna   A colleague? Not yet.

Cora (*smiling*)   I like my job.

Anna   I like my job too, I'd just like it better if we could get rid of some of this sexual tension.

Cora   You think having sex will get rid of the sexual tension?

Anna   I didn't say anything about sex, that was you.

Beat.

Cora   I don't think our politics align.

Anna   Sorry? (*Realising she's serious.*) Are you serious?

Cora   Yeah.

Anna   And what are my politics?

Cora   I know you're very pro-government.

Anna   You don't actually know that. Because you've never asked me.

Cora   I've heard.

Anna   Who did you hear from?

Cora   Stephen told me, the other day.

Anna   You were enquiring?

Cora   It came up.

Anna   It just came up did it?

Cora   It did.

Anna   But sure Stephen's the National Alliance nut.

Cora   That was news to me as well.

Anna   So what did he say about me?

Cora   He said you were pro-Health and Wellness Act. And that you voted National Alliance /

Anna   So on that very solid information, you're gone off me now?

Cora   I just don't think I could go out with someone who would vote for fascists and racists.

Anna   You're joking?

Cora   They banned food. Half the country is starving, you said it yourself you can't believe we're still open. And for all their rhetoric about openness and equality they're clearly racist.

Anna   Where are you getting that from?

Cora   Anna, Mason's cousin was shot last month.

Anna   He was robbing a post office.

Cora   He was unarmed.

Anna   Well I wasn't there so I'm not going to speak on that.

Cora   So what about Eadie's sister? And the other eight Junk Advocates missing.

Anna   Oh my God. You're a conspiracy theorist.

Cora   Do you really think these are all coincidences?

Anna   Look if you didn't like me you could have just said.

Cora   I do like you but I also think you're a fascist.

Mason (*Sous Chef*) *enters through the back door and makes a beeline for the door to the dining room.*

Mason   Is Aidan in there?

Anna   Yeah. (*Pointing towards the dining room.*)

Mason   Thanks.

Cora   Mason, how's Eadie?

Mason   She's downstairs.

Anna   She's not?

Mason   I know. Don't talk to me.

Mason *walks into the dining room.*

Beat.

Anna   Nice to know you made a decision on me, without actually talking to me.

Waiter **Stephen** *and Kitchen Porter* **Anthony** *enter through the back door.*

Cora *walks over to the dining room door and gives* **Aidan** *a nod through the window.*

Anthony   Eadie's downstairs.

Cora   We heard.

Anthony   Cora, she shouldn't be in.

Cora   What do you want me to do? Do you want me to tell her to go home?

Anthony   No. But, (*to* **Stephen**) am I wrong?

Stephen   I don't know. Maybe she needs a distraction.

Anthony   Well I don't think she should be here.

Anna   We heard you Anthony.

Eadie *walks through the back door.*

Cora   Hi love.

Eadie   Hi.

Anna   How are you?

Eadie   Em. (*Shrugs.*) Fine.

Anthony   Are you alright being here?

Cora   Anthony shut up.

Anthony   I'm only asking.

Eadie   I'm grand. Thanks.

Anthony   Will you let us know if you need anything?

Eadie   I'd love to just act normal, if we could.

Aidan *and* **Mason** *enter.*

Aidan   Jesus, Eadie. You are in.

Eadie   I am in yeah.

Aidan (*to* **Mason**)   Why did you let her come in?

Mason   It's nothing to do with me.

Eadie   Aidan, he's my boyfriend, he's not my carer.

Aidan   Right, yeah, no of course. Em. We were all very sorry, to eh. Hear about Lila, about your sister passing. Are you alright to be in?

Eadie   I would really appreciate the distraction, Aidan, so if we could just crack on.

Stephen (*to* **Anthony**)   That's exactly what I said.

Aidan   Stephen shut up. OK. Well. Right, listen up. We've a full house tonight.

Stephen   Waaay!

Aidan   I know. I got a phone call this morning and we've been asked to host some of the National Alliance for dinner, including the President and the Vice President.

A ringing noise in **Eadie***'s ears. The colour drains from her face.*

Aidan*'s next few lines are muffled.*

Aidan   Now I know this is out of the blue and that we haven't had a big booking in a while but I fully believe we can do this. If we work together and knuckle down, I know we can really make a good impression here tonight.

Aidan *notices* **Eadie** *looks faint.*

Ringing noise stops.

Aidan   Eadie? Are you alright?

Eadie   I'm fine.

Mason   Do you want to sit down?

Eadie   I'm fine, I just haven't eaten.

Aidan   Maybe, maybe you should sit tonight out? It's a lot of pressure for your first shift back.

Eadie   I'm fine.

Beat.

Aidan   OK. Em. They've asked to book the place out so Anna I need you to cancel the covers we have.

Anna   Sorry? What am I supposed to tell people?

Aidan   You can tell them the place burned down for all I care, just cancel them.

Mason   And hang on, are they happy to order off our menu? Because I can't get anything else in, we got our allowance for the week already.

Aidan   They are happy to order off our menu, with a few minor alterations, first can everyone sign this NDA please?

Aidan *motions to the paper in his hand.*

Anna   What?

Cora   Give us a look.

Aidan (*passing the NDAs out*)   It's fairly standard. You can't tell anyone they're here, no pictures and they want our phones before service.

Anna   Aidan, I'm not giving you my phone.

Aidan   Well you don't have to sign it if you don't want to work tonight. Stephen can handle the floor.

Stephen   Absolutely I can handle the floor.

Anna   Would you jump in my grave as quick?

Stephen   You're the one who doesn't want to hand over your phone.

Anna   I'm your manager, you're supposed to stick up for me.

Stephen   All due respect, Anna, I couldn't give a fuck who you are.

Aidan   OK that's enough Stephen.

Anna   Aidan, I didn't say I wouldn't sign it.

Aidan   Good. So sign it. Look I know this seems like a pain in the hole but it's an honour. Plus we'll be booked up til next year if this goes well. And we need that.

Everyone reads the NDAs, signs and passes them back to **Aidan**.

Aidan   Phones.

Everyone passes their phones to **Aidan**.

Aidan   Right, menu alterations, Mason, can we do a mustard and caper sauce on the celeriac steak. Cora, they've asked for blackened Cajun sweet potatoes, you look after them. Fruit plates for dessert. And em. Eadie, we have to make some caramel. And they want it made with sugar.

Beat.

Eadie   What?

Aidan   Yeah.

Eadie   Sugar?

Anthony   Real sugar?

Aidan   Real sugar.

Eadie   Sugar? Who wants it made with sugar? How much caramel?

Aidan   One portion. For the President.

Mason   Breaking his own law?

Cora   That is gas.

Eadie   So caramel for one?

Aidan   You happy enough to do that?

Eadie   I haven't cooked with sugar in a year.

Stephen (*under his breath*)   Yeah right.

Aidan   Stephen, you're getting on my nerves, shut up.

Eadie   Who's this coming from?

Aidan   Direct order from the Chief of Staff.

Eadie   Aidan if anyone found out we were working with sugar /

Aidan   You just signed a non-disclosure agreement. So they won't find out. And Eadie, you can't taste it.

Eadie   Ah that is ridiculous, Aidan. How am I supposed to make something I can't taste?

Aidan   I don't know Eadie but with the greatest respect in the world, if you're not up to it, someone else can do it.

Eadie   No I can do it.

Aidan   OK good. They have an interview set up with Oisín Ó Hanluain straight after dinner so their team is coming over early to set up a camera and lights in the dining room. Can you look after that Stephen?

Stephen   With pleasure.

Aidan   OK. Any questions?

Silence.

Aidan   Well then let's get cracking. Don't mess this up.

Everyone snaps into action.

Anna   Stephen, bring up that big box of silver cutlery from the basement and polish it.

Stephen (*sarcastically*)   Right boss.

Stephen *goes downstairs.*

Anna   Prick.

Anna *goes into the dining room and* **Aidan** *goes to follow her.*

Eadie   Aidan, where are we getting the sugar from?

Aidan   Anthony will get it, Anthony?

Anthony   Yes Chef?

Aidan *gives him a slip of paper.*

Aidan   You can pick up the sugar, butter and cream from there. Don't be long.

Anthony   Yes Chef.

Aidan *walks into the dining room.*

Anthony *is looking at the list and walking out when* **Eadie** *stops him.*

Anthony   You alright?

Eadie   Can you pick something up for me?

Anthony   OK, let me get a pen.

Anthony *pats his empty pockets.*

Eadie   You don't need a pen, I just need one thing.

Anthony   What is it?

Eadie   Rat poison.

Anthony   Do we have none here?

Eadie   We're out. I saw a rat.

Anthony   Today?

Eadie   About a half an hour ago.

Anthony   What, where?

Eadie   In the locker room.

Anthony   But my coat is down there.

Eadie   I don't think he wants your coat Anthony. Just get some. And don't tell anyone.

Anthony   OK.

Eadie   When you come back just give it to me on the sly with the sugar and I'll handle it.

Anthony   Yeah fine. Are you sure you're alright Eadie?

Eadie   I'm grand.

Anthony *leaves through the back door and* **Aidan** *comes back into the kitchen. Everyone is getting to work and a lightbulb in the kitchen blows.*

Aidan   Great.

Eight: Vvvvvvvvvvvvvvvvv

Mr Costello's *office – ten months ago.*

A fisheye lens being tapped on.

Stephen *is wearing a camera disguised as a pin on his shirt.* **Mr Kelly** *is looking into the lens.*

Mr Kelly   You can't even see that. Technology!

Stephen   And will it make a sound?

Mr Kelly   What kind of sound?

Stephen   I don't know. Like a vvvvvvvvvvvvvvvvv

Tiny pause.

Mr Kelly   No.

Stephen   Oh GOOD.

Mr Kelly   It shouldn't.

Stephen   Phew.

Mr Kelly   Exciting isn't it?

Stephen   It is exciting. I'm a bit nervous too, to be honest though.

Mr Kelly   What's there to be nervous about? (*Tapping the camera again.*) This little guy will do all the work for you. You just have to be completely normal and speak with absolute clarity.

Stephen   Just I suppose you wonder, don't you, is it a bit wrong? Recording people without their knowledge.

Mr Kelly   If they're not doing anything wrong, they've nothing to be worried about.

Stephen   No. No you're dead right.

Mr Kelly   And if they are doing something wrong, they deserve to be punished. Right?

Stephen   They do, I agree with that 100 per cent sir, yeah. And you're not going to use the footage for anything weird?

Mr Kelly   Listen, you have no idea how many people we have consulting for us. You're not even the only one in your restaurant.

Stephen   Really? Who else?

Mr Kelly   I can't tell you that.

Stephen   Why not?

Mr Kelly   Because then I'd have to kill you.

Stephen   Ha!

Mr Kelly *doesn't laugh.*

Mr Kelly   Look this isn't anything sinister, with this new Act coming in we just need eyes and ears on the ground. The country is still in a transitional period but we really want this to work. It's important for a government to listen to its people. Even if it is surreptitiously.

Stephen   Yeah. I agree with that as well. Here, did I ever tell you I did the police entrance exam? Twice. Didn't get it, but I came close. Did I ever tell you?

Mr Kelly   You did.

Mr Costello *enters*.

Mr Costello   Afternoon Mr Kelly.

Mr Kelly   Good afternoon Mr Costello.

Mr Costello   Who do we have here?

Mr Kelly   This is our man in The Royal Marine.

Mr Costello   Oh of course, well, pleasure.

Stephen   Pleasure's all mine sir.

Mr Costello   Aidan Proctor's your Head Chef there.

Stephen   He is.

Mr Kelly   The absolute bastard.

Stephen   Good chef though.

Mr Costello   You can let go of the compulsory compliments lad. They're not necessary here.

Stephen   Sure. Yeah. He is a bit of a bastard actually.

Mr Costello   That's the spirit. Easy though, we know Aidan well.

Stephen   Is he working for you too?

Mr Kelly   Mum's the word.

Stephen   I never knew, what does that mean?

Mr Kelly   No idea, now obviously there are things in the kitchen that we won't see.

Mr Costello   Exactly, so we'd also like reports from you directly.

Stephen   Wow, yeah absolutely. How often?

Mr Kelly   Daily.

Stephen   Daily? Yes. Fantastic. What sort of stuff are you looking for?

Mr Kelly   Anything that feels off.

Mr Costello   Anything at all really. We want you to trust your gut.

Mr Kelly   That's why we chose you.

Stephen   I'm honoured to be chosen. And should I email these reports?

Mr Costello   No no. Unlike our predecessors we don't trust the internet.

Mr Kelly   Not with all the psychos on there.

Mr Costello   Everything important is handwritten.

Stephen   Understood. (*To* **Mr Costello**.) I don't know if Mr Kelly told you sir but I did the police entrance exam a few years ago. Twice.

Mr Costello   Where did you come?

Stephen   It was a very tough year I believe. I was 174.

Mr Costello   Well. If you do a good job for us I don't see why you can't be bumped up a notch.

Stephen   Really sir?

Mr Costello   What do you think, Mr Kelly?

Mr Kelly *puts his arm around* **Stephen** *and they turn to face a mirror.*

Mr Kelly   I think Stephen would make a fine addition to the Police force.

Mr Costello   I agree.

Mr Kelly   Stephen in your dealings with us you'll be operating under a pseudonym.

Stephen   Like a code name? Like Night Rider or something?

Mr Kelly   Sort of like that but also nothing like that at all.

Mr Costello   I was thinking of something unassuming.

Mr Kelly   Tom?

Mr Costello   We have a Tom.

Mr Kelly   Oh Karl? With a K.

Mr Costello   Perfect.

Stephen   Karl.

Mr Costello   Karl.

Stephen   I will not let you down sirs.

Mr Kelly   That's it Karl. Just keep your eyes open.

Jump forward in time to the present day.

We can see through the fisheye lens on **Stephen**'*s top, he's carrying a box of silverware through the kitchen and into the dining room.*

Nine: Mortar Part I

Eadie'*s eyes.*

A ringing sound.

CUT TO: A video on social media.

Lila, *indoors and smiling. The light is cooler than before and* **Lila** *looks pale.*

Caption/VO   What I eat in a day as a person who eats whatever the fuck they want.

The following is an insight into **Eadie**'*s thoughts.*

Lila   For breakfast I miss you so much that it hurts. I've had the wind knocked out of me. Where were you? Eadie what happened? Fight back. CREAM. I lost a fingernail. Chocolate. Fight back. Eadie, I'm in the boot of a car.

CUT TO: Light coming on in the kitchen, **Mason** *is on a ladder having just screwed the bulb back in.*

The kitchen, buzzing with activity. **Anthony** *is standing next to* **Eadie**.

Anthony   Eadie?

Eadie   Yeah, sorry.

Anthony   Here. Are you positive you're alright?

Anthony *hands her two plastic bags, one with 1kg of sugar, butter and cream, the other with rat poison.*

Eadie   I wish everyone would stop asking me that. Thank you. (*She looks in the bag.*) Hey wait, these are pellets.

Anthony   That's all they had. They're really strong though so your man said we don't need to use a lot.

Eadie   Did they not have powder?

Anthony   No.

Anthony *is still for a moment.*

Eadie *is holding back her distress.*

Eadie   I thought it would be powder.

Pause.

Anthony *looks at the bag with the pellets in it.*

He swiftly takes out a large stone pestle and mortar out of a nearby press and puts it on **Eadie**'s *table.*

Aidan   Anthony, c'mere.

Anthony *walks over to* **Aidan** *and they both go into the dining room.*

Eadie *hurriedly takes out weighing scales and a large deep pan. She looks around and when she sees no one looking at her she throws two handfuls of pellets into the mortar and starts crushing them. Half-way through she measures the sugar and mixes them together.*

CUT TO: A video on social media.

Lila, *indoors and smiling. The light is grey and* **Lila**'s *voice is slightly frantic.*

Caption/VO   Recipe for lethal caramel.

Lila (*V/O*)   Today we're going to make some lethal caramel to avenge my death – LET'S GO. Medium heat, two cups of sugar, a quarter cup of water, two tablespoons of ground rat poison and bring it to the boil. Add one cup of heavy cream and one stick of butter. That's really going to counteract that bitter aftertaste rat poison sometimes has. Add a teaspoon of salt, some vanilla extract and because we're not entirely sure we used enough rat poison for a lethal dose, let's add some household chemicals; lighter fluid, furniture polish and bleach. Also some nail glue remover I had in my bag that I heard contained cyanide. Cook until the thermometer reaches 240°F then leave to cool.

Eadie *laughs.*

CUT TO: The kitchen, everyone staring at **Eadie**.

Mason   Eadie?

Eadie   What?

Mason   Are you alright?

Eadie   I'm fine. Are you alright?

Mason   Not really.

Eadie   Why?

Mason   You've barely said one word to me since Lila was found.

Eadie   What did you want me to say?

Mason   I don't want you to say anything. Can I do anything for you?

Eadie   Jesus, Mason.

Mason   No seriously. Solutions or comfort?

Eadie   Neither.

Mason   OK.

Eadie *moves away from him.*

Mason   Eadie, I don't know what to do. You haven't even cried.

Eadie   Excuse me?

Mason   It's not a normal reaction to your sister /

Eadie   How would you know?

Mason *is surprised at the tone in* **Eadie***'s voice.*

Eadie   I'm sorry Mason but your cousin isn't the same.

Mason   That feels, cruel.

Eadie   I don't mean it to be cruel.

Mason   I'm really trying here. Can you see that?

Eadie   Yes.

Mason   I think we should go home.

Eadie   The two of us? Aidan'll hit the roof.

Mason   We don't need to be here, there's five people coming for dinner, the caramel's made. Literally Cora and Aidan could do this by themselves.

Eadie   Mason, I need to be in work.

Mason   It's too soon for you to be in work. I'll come home with you, please, let's just go.

Eadie   Why?

Mason   Because I'm afraid.

Anthony *enters the kitchen.*

Eadie   Of what?

Mason   I feel like something bad is going to happen.

Eadie   Mason, I don't want to make decisions based on your feelings.

Mason   Did you hear what you just said?

Eadie   I need to stay here tonight.

Mason   Why?

Eadie   You're just worried I might freak out and make a show of you.

Mason   No I'm not. Have you considered that I want to go because I don't want to be here?

Eadie   Why wouldn't you want to be here? This is a huge deal for the restaurant.

Mason   I'm not exactly keen on drawing attention to myself. In case you haven't noticed I'm not from here.

Aidan *enters the kitchen.*

Eadie   What has that got to do with anything?

Mason   There are government officials coming here tonight. My ability to remain in this country is not as permanent as yours.

Eadie   They're not going to look in the kitchen, Mason.

Mason   Look we haven't been together very long and I can't describe – I can't tell you how sorry I am for what happened to Lila. But you don't know what it's like for me.

Eadie   What is it like?

Mason   My cousin was shot here, Eadie. Look, I don't want to have this conversation now.

Eadie   I understand why you want to go and I do think they are racist / but I

Aidan   Who's a racist?

Mason   No one.

Eadie   The National Alliance.

Aidan   That's impossible. Irish people can't be racists.

Everyone stops, mostly baffled at what **Aidan** *has said.*

Anthony   Wha?

Eadie *goes to the corner of the kitchen and stands trying to catch her breath.*

Eadie*'s eyes.*

A ringing sound.

Catching Her Breath

A memory.

Eadie *is in her own home, early morning, before* **Lila** *disappeared.*

Eadie (*desperately trying to understand*)   And, I'm sorry. Are you OK with this?

Lila   What's the question? Am I OK with death threats or my details being posted online. What are you asking?

Eadie   Don't be smart.

Lila   I'm not being smart, what are you asking?

Eadie   Someone has been to your house, Lila. They know your address. Are you joking?

Lila   Well I don't know what to do about that.

Eadie   This is serious. If this is the response you're getting from the internet, why keep doing it? Why put yourself out there? You're making yourself available to violence.

Lila   So I should be more like you?

Eadie   That's not what I'm saying.

Lila   Should I squirrel away in secret and not talk about anything?

Eadie   No, no but the way I operate / is

Lila   Eadie, the way you operate is quietly. You're happy to disagree, to continue using sugar and whatever on the quiet.

Eadie   But the way I operate, I get very few death threats.

Lila   I don't know what you want me to say.

Eadie   You share too much online and I just don't think it's worth all this anger.

Lila   I think the banning of foods is the start of something very dangerous. And it's / the

Eadie   Well it is very dangerous for you now. Because you go on the internet and you tell everybody what you're eating and you draw attention to yourself, you actually pull focus onto you and I'm worried, Lila, I'm worried about you.

Lila   OK, OK, I know, I know.

Eadie   I don't understand why you have to be the one to stick your head above the parapet.

Lila   And I don't understand why you don't want to stick your head above the parapet. (*Pause.*) What is a parapet?

Eadie   It's like a protective, (*does a little 'over' gesture*) it's a structure.

Lila   Oh right. (*Brief pause.*) I'm not the only one doing it.

Eadie   Can you take a break?

Lila   Not really no /

Eadie   Please?

Lila   I don't want to.

Eadie   'Cause your 'fans' will miss you?

Lila   Eadie, I love you but I don't agree with you.

Eadie   Can you stay here again tonight please?

Lila   Yes. Let me go home and grab some stuff.

*The rest of the conversation is muffled as **Eadie**'s focus is pulled back into the kitchen.*

Lila   Everything's going to be OK. I'll report everything.

Eadie   You should have reported it yesterday.

Lila   Do you want pancakes for dinner?

Eadie   Yes.

Lila   Do we need anything?

Eadie   Milk and eggs.

Lila   OK. Eadie? Everything's fine.

Eadie   Everything's fine.

Nine: Mortar Part II

Eadie *is back in the kitchen.*

Aidan   All I'm saying is because we were colonised by the British Empire and made indentured servants /

Cora   Are you comparing that to slavery?

Anthony   Aidan, seriously?

Aidan   It's the same, it's just history. Mason, we're the same.

Cora   Holy shit.

Mason   We are not the same.

Aidan   Mason, you know I'm not a racist.

Mason   I know you couldn't possibly assess whether Ireland is racist or not. We're not the same.

Aidan   Well maybe / I

Mason   No you couldn't. For one, you don't personally know everyone in Ireland. So you can't speak on the prejudices of people you don't know.

Aidan   But neither can you.

Mason   OK, but being a white man, you don't know what it's like to have black skin.

Aidan   So?

Mason   So racists wouldn't necessarily treat you differently.

Aidan   But they might tell me that they're a racist.

Mason   Why am I explaining myself to you?

Aidan   Take it easy Mason.

Mason   Fuck you Aidan.

Mason *walks out of the kitchen and knocks an empty pot off the counter on his way out.*

Aidan   In my own kitchen, today of all days.

Aidan *walks over to* **Eadie***'s station with a spoon in his hand.*

Eadie   What are you doing?

Aidan   Eadie don't start, is this the caramel?

Eadie   Yes, but / you're not.

Aidan   OK.

Aidan *dips his spoon in to taste it.*

The ringing sound in **Eadie***'s ears starts again. It gets louder and louder over the next few lines.*

Eadie   Aidan, you're not supposed to taste it.

Aidan   Eadie, honestly this night is too important to mess up. I'm not trying to say I don't trust you, but I need this to go well. They're not going to find out if I taste it.

Eadie *walks back over to her station.*

Eadie   Aidan don't.

Aidan   Eadie this is my kitchen.

Aidan *raises the spoon to his lips.*

Eadie *picks up the large stone mortar and cracks* **Aidan** *over the head with it.*

The ringing sound stops the second the mortar comes into contact with his skull.

He falls to the ground and a small pool of blood begins spilling from his head.

Cora, **Mason** *and* **Anthony** *are horrified.*

Ten: Some Heat

(*This scene may happen simultaneously to* **Eleven: What Did You Do?** *stopping just before* **Anna** *enters.*)

The all-white room is empty.

Suddenly the door is kicked open and two men, **Guard One** *and* **Guard Two**, *enter, both wearing masks.*

Guard One *is carrying* **Margot** *over his shoulder, her wrists and ankles are bound and she is wearing a gag. She has just tried to escape.*

Guard Two *is carrying a small black case and a plastic bag with something heavy in it.*

Guard One *sits* **Margot** *down on a chair.*

Guard Two *takes an electric razor and a tweezers out of the case.*

Guard One *gently pushes* **Margot***'s head forward so her chin touches her chest.*

Guard Two *turns on the electric razor in her hand and begins shaving* **Margot***'s head.*

Margot *doesn't move.*

Then they shave her eyebrows.

They pluck out her eyelashes.

When **Guard Two** *is finished shaving,* **Guard One** *takes a hammer out of the bag and* **Guard Two** *holds* **Margot***'s right leg.* **Guard One** *brings the hammer down sharply on* **Margot***'s knee and she screams in anguish, still gagged. They do the same to her left. Then they leave.*

Eleven: What Did You Do?

(*This scene may happen simultaneously to* **Ten: Some Heat**)

The kitchen staff all stand around **Aidan***'s still body.*

Mason *comes back in the kitchen.*

Cora   Eadie, what the fuck did you do?

Mason   What the fuck did who do?

Eadie   Mason, get his legs.

Mason   Eadie?

Cora   Why did you do that?

Mason *checks* **Aidan***'s pulse.*

Eadie   Is he breathing?

Mason   Yes.

Mason *puts his head in his hands.*

Cora   Thank God.

Mason   I think.

Eadie   That's good.

Cora   That's OK? Anthony, call an ambulance.

Eadie   No.

Cora   Eadie you're not well /

Eadie   You have no idea what he said about my sister.

Mason   Aidan?

Anthony   He was going to taste the caramel.

Mason   What does that mean?

Anthony   She said there was a rat, I didn't know /

Eadie   I think he killed my sister.

Mason   What?

Eadie   Martin. He called her a bitch, they had her address /

Mason   OK calm down. How do you know that?

Anthony   I'm going to go to jail.

Eadie   No you're not.

Anthony   Yes I am.

Eadie   No you're not, it was me. You didn't see anything.

Anthony   I did though. I saw you hit him in the head.

Cora   Eadie this isn't happening, we need to call an ambulance.

Eadie   Please. Please, can we just not doing anything until after dinner, just until then please.

Cora   Aidan needs to go to hospital.

Eadie   Aidan's fine.

They all look at **Aidan**.

He's not fine.

He starts to groan and wake up.

Eadie   Look, there, he's up. Can we please just move him downstairs and then we can talk, just let's put him downstairs, and get him water, before Anna or Stephen come in because you know, an ambulance won't be their first call.

Breath.

Cora   Alright. Let's move him downstairs. Anthony, you stay with Aidan until Eadie and I talk. Then we're calling an ambulance.

Mason   Anthony, grab his arms.

Anthony   No.

Cora   Aidan love, we're just going to pick you up.

Aidan *groans.*

Mason   Please, Anthony.

Anthony   Absolutely no way.

Eadie   I'll do it.

Anthony   I can't breathe.

Cora (*getting a mop*)   Anthony, relax.

Eadie   Put him in the freezer, they'll check the break room.

Cora   Oh my god.

Mason   I'll go first.

Eadie *and* **Mason** *pick* **Aidan** *up and* **Mason** *manoeuvres his way towards the back door. They are right beside the dining room door when* **Anna** *walks in.*

They freeze.

Anthony   Anna this wasn't me.

Anna *looks at* **Cora**.

She steps back and opens the dining room door.

Anna   Stephen?

Anthony   I'm going to have a heart attack.

Anna   Stephen, take the brush and go sweep out the front.

Stephen (*O.S*) (*quietly*)   Bitch.

Anna *turns back to the kitchen.*

Anna   Go.

Mason *kicks the back door open with his foot and they drag* **Aidan** *out.*

Anthony   Should we call the police?

Cora   Anthony, just help clean. Anna?

Cora *throws her a tea towel and* **Anna** *starts cleaning up the blood trail.*

Anna   What happened?

Anthony   She just attacked Aidan. She just hit him over the head.

Anna   Why?

Cora   I don't know.

Anthony   He was going to taste the caramel.

The phone starts to ring.

Anthony, **Cora** *and* **Anna** *freeze.*

Cora   Answer it.

Anthony   Honestly Cora, get fucked, I'm the last person that should be answering the kitchen phone.

Cora   Well do something.

The phone rings out.

Mason *enters from the back door.*

Stephen *sticks his head in the side door.*

Stephen   Hey. Why didn't you pick up the phone?

Mason   What?

Stephen   What's wrong?

Cora   I spilled a pot of stock.

Mason   Everything is fine, we cleaned it. What's up?

Stephen (*excitedly*)   The National Alliance are here!

Mason   What?

Stephen   Yeah and the President is here! It's brilliant. He's so handsome.

Mason   Why?

Stephen   I don't know but he looks great.

Mason   No, why are they here now?

Stephen   They're early.

Anthony   You're joking?

Stephen   What's the problem? The restaurant is booked out for them?

Eadie *enters.*

Eadie   Hi Stephen.

Mason   The National Alliance are here. In the dining room.

Eadie   What?

Mason   Stephen they're not due for another five hours.

Stephen   So what? I'm not going to tell them to leave.

There is an air of panic in the kitchen.

Stephen   Are youz alright?

Mason   We're fine. OK, we're fine. Stephen, you'll have to tell them dinner won't be ready for two hours.

Stephen   I think they just want to drink for a while.

Eadie   I can't believe they're early.

Stephen   It's not that unbelievable.

Anthony   I sort of feel like I'm going to pass out. Do you know that feeling? When you feel like you're going to faint? Or die? Could I be dying?

Stephen   Where is Aidan?

Beat.

Eadie   He got a phone call. He had to leave.

Stephen   What? When?

Cora (*reluctantly*)   About ten minutes ago.

Stephen   Shit. They want to come in and say hello to him.

Eadie   Well he's not here.

Stephen   Can I let them in anyway?

Eadie *and* **Cora**   No.

Stephen   Eh. If the President wants to come in the kitchen, I'm going to let him in the kitchen.

Anthony   I mean my actual nose isn't working, like no air is getting in.

Eadie   OK fine, let them in but can you give us a minute, Stephen?

Stephen   Sure.

Stephen *leaves.*

Mason   OK. OK. OK, OK, OK.

Eadie   You're OK, we're OK, just breathe. Anthony, by the sink. Everyone else, pick a station and stay there. Be busy. Smile. Anna, let them in.

Anna *leaves and almost immediately the door swings back open and* **Sanbrooke**, **Cordelia**, **Ava**, **Mr Kelly** *enter briskly. They occupy the space as if they own it. The temperature in the room changes.*

All the kitchen staff freeze at their stations.

Cordelia   Well. Look at all the kitchen people. Is Aidan here?

Mason   I'm Mason.

Cordelia   That's great. I'm looking for Aidan.

Mason   I'm the Sous Chef, Aidan is the Head Chef.

Cordelia   Uh-huh. And where is the Head Chef?

Mason   He's had to step out. Urgent phone call. I can look after you.

Cordelia   That's unprofessional. The President is here.

Sanbrooke   That's fine, Cordelia, I'm sure this chap knows his way around the kitchen. (*Loudly.*) Hello sir!

Cordelia (*smiling*)   OK. I suppose we'll start. (*To* **Ava**.) Ava, the stand.

Ava *quickly unfolds a tiny step ladder which* **Cordelia** *steps up on.*

Cordelia *gathers herself.*

Cordelia   Hi there. I'm Cordelia, Press Secretary for the National Alliance Party, obviously. I know we're a little early but we couldn't wait to get the celebrations underway. And the President, in his infinite wisdom /

Sanbrooke   Get on with it.

Cordelia   Mmk, the President just wanted to pop in and say hello to you all.

She dismounts the step ladder. **Sanbrooke** *kicks it out of the way and* **Ava** *hurriedly picks it up.*

Sanbrooke   I don't want the ladder. Good afternoon, it's a real pleasure to meet some real people. We can't wait to see what you have been cooking up for us!

Sanbrooke *dismounts and* **Cordelia** *starts a clap that everyone joins in on.*

Cordelia   Fantastic speech, really moving sir. So who's who here?

Mason   Eh, I'm Mason, this is Cora, Chef de Partie, Anna is our Restaurant Manager, Anthony is our Kitchen Porter and Eadie is, em, our Pâtissier.

Cordelia   Fantastic.

Mason   And Stephen /

Mr Kelly   Oh we've met Stephen.

Cordelia   I will be floating around setting up for an interview after dinner but we'll let you guys get back to it for now. Exciting.

All the kitchen staff go back to working in complete silence.

Sanbrooke *is walking out and a thread from his jacket gets caught on a drawer handle.* **Mr Kelly** *removes his hunting knife from its sheath and cuts the thread in full view of everyone in the kitchen.*

Sanbrooke   Thank you Mr Kelly.

They go into the dining room. **Stephen** *follows them.*

Stephen   Drinks gentlemen?

Cordelia   Ava, quick word.

Ava   Sure.

Cordelia   Yeah, so you're fired.

Ava   What?

Cordelia   You promised us the Head Chef would be here to personally look after the President.

Ava   I don't know where he is.

Cordelia   Oh I don't care. You had one job, book the dinner. And you scuppered it up. You're done.

Beat.

Ava   Oh fuck you.

Cordelia   Excuse me?

Ava   Fuck you. You are a vapid, stuck up, spineless nothing of a woman. You're a nightmare to work for and it would be my pleasure to never see you again.

Ava *leaves.*

Cordelia *looks up at the smirking kitchen staff. She turns and leaves.*

Cordelia   Rude.

Twelve: Something Nice

Margot *is sitting in a wheelchair in the all-white room with her legs bandaged up.*

Her head shaved.

The door opens.

Guard One *and* **Guard Two** *step in, wearing masks.*

They are each carrying large cases, which they set down.

Margot *doesn't move.*

Guard Two *wheels in a rack of clothes and shoes.*

Guard One *opens his case and takes out a selection of wigs, makeup and jewellery. He also gives* **Margot** *a script to memorise.*

Guard Two *opens his case and ceremoniously takes out the actual shoes from* Midnight Forever.

He places them on her and both guards clap with excitement.

Guard One *begins to do* **Margot**'s *makeup with great skill.*

Guard Two *picks out her clothes and hands her a small bag containing her inhaler.*

When she is ready, **Margot** *is wheeled into the dining room of the restaurant by the* **Guards**.

Chapter Three: Dessert

Thirteen: What Fray Was Here

A news report.

Text in the lower third left-hand side of the screen reads 'Oisín Ó Hanluain – TDT News'

Oisín This evening The National Alliance Party celebrates the anniversary of the Health and Wellness Act. To mark the event, they have held a star-studded party at The Royal Marine.

Split screen of news report and live feed with **Cordelia**. *She's on her camera phone, in a darkened room and there's smoke coming from off camera. She looks manic and her hair is wild but she's trying to keep her cool.*

Oisín We haven't been invited but we go live there now where the Press Secretary Cordelia Flowers is with, oh Ms Flowers you're alone. Is the party getting out of hand?

Cordelia A little.

Oisín We were expecting you to be with BAFTA winner Margot Murphy.

Cordelia (*smiling maniacally*) Well it's just me, Osh.

Oisín *notices* **Cordelia**'*s face is speckled with blood.*

Oisín Em. Good evening Ms Flowers, looking ravishing as always. Is that blood on your face?

Cordelia Thank you, Oisín, yes it is.

Oisín *looks bamboozled.*

Oisín Ms Flowers. Where is Ms Murphy?

Cordelia Em. (*Pause.*) She's dead.

Beat.

Oisín   I beg your pardon?

Cordelia   She's dead.

Oisín   What happened?

Cordelia   Well after dinner, there was eh, there was a fray of sorts and, I think, quite a lot of them are dead actually.

Beat.

Oisín   This is breaking news from inside The Royal Marine restaurant where a government celebration has turned into a bloodbath, Cordelia, would it be fair to say it was a bloodbath?

Cordelia (*shaky*)   I think that would be fair to say.

Oisín   Ms Flowers can you give us the status of the President?

Cordelia (*very distressed*)   The President, no, he didn't make it.

Oisín   Are you saying the President is dead?

Cordelia   I am.

Oisín   Breaking news, President Sanbrooke Martin is dead. Ms Flowers can you describe to us what happened?

Cordelia   There's been an assassination attempt, success, em. We think some disgruntled supporter of the President's slit . . . his throat was slit.

Oisín   His throat was slit?

Cordelia   That's right Oisín.

Oisín *recalibrates.*

Oisín   Cordelia those cameras that you have, were they recording before dinner?

Cordelia   Unfortunately they've been damaged.

Oisín   OK Cordelia, sit tight, we're sending someone down.

Cordelia   The police are on their way.

Oisín   Of course they are.

Cordelia   Can you call my mum please?

Oisín's *excitement wanes for a moment.*

Oisín   Sure, yes, we can.

Cordelia   Thank you.

Oisín   Cordelia, are you safe?

Cordelia's *picture starts to go.*

Oisín   Cordelia?

Cordelia's *picture is lost.*

Oisín   Ms Flowers?

No response.

Oisín (*to someone behind the camera*)   Get someone down there.

CUT TO: **Eadie**'s *eyes.*

A ringing sound.

CUT TO: A video on social media.

Lila, *indoors and stony faced.*

Comment on screen: 'You deserve to get raped and die. See you soon'.

Lila (*V/O*)   I need to address some of the comments and messages I've been getting recently. I've received messages from people saying that the work I do promotes obesity, promotes cancer, that because I acquire illegal foods that I am a bitch or a whore, weirdly. I've gotten death threats, rape threats, everything, and I wasn't planning on talking like this but I'm just going to say it because I'm shadow banned anyway so it doesn't matter. Let me be clear. This is not about food. This is about control. Our government, our elected officials, want to control us. By banning certain foods and restricting what we can consume, they are removing our right to choose. And vilifying the people publicly working to reinstate that right. I am not your enemy. I'm not stuffing my face with chocolate to make you mad. OK? I don't like my rights being taken away. And all this hate is intended to make me back down, I understand that. But what it is actually doing is letting me know I'm having an effect. I'm making someone's job very very difficult. Someone is noticing me. Isn't that right? Why else would you post my address online? They are restricting what goes into our mouths, they are trying to restrict what comes out of my mouth and they will do the same to you. Are you going to let them?

Fourteen: Butter Me Up and Cover Me In Caramel

A banquet table – After dinner but before dessert.

There is a table to the side on which sits a magnum of champagne in an ice bucket, a bottle of expensive vodka and a box of cutlery.

Kitchen door is closest to the **Mr Costello** *and there is another door at the back of the room.* **Margot** *is in a wheelchair.* **Sanbrooke** *has clearly been drinking for some time.* **Cordelia** *and* **Stephen** *are hovering. Everyone seated is drinking champagne, except* **Mr Costello** *who is drinking vodka.*

Suggested seating plan:

Mr Costello   Jana   Sanbrooke   Margot   Mr Kelly

Sanbrooke   A toast to the world's best actor!

Jana   Absolutely.

Mr Costello   Hear hear!

They toast. **Sanbrooke** *spills some of his down the front of his shirt.*

Margot *passes him a napkin.*

Sanbrooke   This glass doesn't work.

Stephen   I'll get you a new one sir.

Stephen *runs into the kitchen.*

Sanbrooke (*to* **Margot**)   You are so lovely.

Margot   Thank you.

Sanbrooke   I have to say Ms Murphy, it is a thrill to have you here, you were so good to come.

Sanbrooke *touches her hair and* **Margot** *flinches.*

Margot   It wasn't entirely my choice.

Sanbrooke   Well I've always been of the opinion that if you give people a choice, they often don't make the right one. And if you hadn't come, we wouldn't have got to see you don that beautiful dress. And those shoes. (*To* **Mr Costello**.) Are those the exact shoes from /

Mr Costello   *Midnight Forever*, they are.

Sanbrooke   *Midnight Forever*, oh my dizzy life!

Stephen *runs back into the dining room with a new glass full of champagne.*

Stephen   Here you go sir.

Sanbrooke   Thank you son.

Jana   Where's Cordelia? Cordelia, can you contact the Producer at TDT and let her know everything set up for the interview?

Cordelia   No problem.

Jana   We can go live with Oisín directly after dessert.

Cordelia *leaves the room to make the call.*

Sanbrooke   Oisín? The reporter?

Jana   I know it's awful, we couldn't get around it sir. Have you seen the embellishment around the toe?

Sanbrooke *looks back down at* **Margot**'s *shoes.*

Mr Costello *taps on his glass.*

Stephen *picks up a bottle of vodka.*

Sanbrooke   They give me shivers, those shoes.

Jana   Sanbrooke, are you ready for dessert?

Sanbrooke   Can I see them?

Sanbrooke *bends down, takes one shoe off* **Margot**, *she flinches again when he touches her.*

Sanbrooke *plonks the heel on the table. It has an impossibly high and sharp stiletto.*

Sanbrooke   Perfect.

Stephen (*to* **Mr Costello**)   More vodka, sir?

Mr Costello   Please.

Jana *lays her hand gently on* **Mr Costello**'s *arm.*

Sanbrooke (*stroking the shoe*)   I mean they're just perfect.

Mr Costello (*to* **Stephen**)   Is the camera ready to go?

Stephen (*to* **Mr Costello**)   On and recording as we speak sir.

Mr Costello   Excellent. (*Louder.*) I think we're ready for dessert now.

Stephen   Yes sir.

Stephen *goes into the kitchen.*

Mr Costello (*to* **Jana**)   Good to go.

Jana   Fantastic.

Sanbrooke   What's fantastic?

Jana   The shoes!

Sanbrooke   I know! I always wanted to wear these shoes. I used to dream about them.

Margot *reluctantly lifts her head to look at the shoe.*

Sanbrooke   I'd dream I was walking down the catwalk, covered in caramel, wearing these shoes. And everyone wanted to lick me.

Jana   Do you want to try them on?

Sanbrooke   No.

Jana   Why not?

Sanbrooke   Because indulging is weak, Jana, you know this, I've told you this.

Jana   Well they really are stunning. Shall we do dessert?

Sanbrooke   Dessert, dessert yes fine fine, bring on the fruit plates.

Stephen *enters with two fruit plates. He lays them down in front of* **Margot** *and* **Mr Kelly** *and re-enters the kitchen.*

Anna *enters carrying another fruit plate and a large clear jug full of caramel. She tentatively sits a plate of fruit in front of* **Sanbrooke** *and puts the caramel down beside it.* **Stephen** *re-enters with fruit plates for* **Jana** *and* **Mr Costello**.

Sanbrooke *is taking a long drink from his glass and as he sets it down, his eyes land on the caramel.*

Sanbrooke   What's that?

Anna   Dessert.

Sanbrooke   And what is dessert?

Jana   Just a sauce for the fruit, Sanbrooke, enjoy it.

Sanbrooke   What kind of sauce is it?

Anna   Em. I'm not sure. Stephen do you /

Stephen   I've never seen that sauce before.

Jana   Just eat it, Sanbrooke, it'll be a surprise. The kitchen knows what they're doing. It's a wonderful restaurant.

Sanbrooke   Get the kitchen staff in here.

Jana *and* **Mr Costello** *look at each other.*

Mr Kelly *instinctively stands up and steps in front of the table.*

Stephen *runs into the kitchen and re-enters followed by* **Mason,** **Cora, Anthony** *and* **Eadie.**

Mr Costello *stands as they enter.*

Anthony *is breathing heavily, obviously distressed.*

Sanbrooke (*gesturing to the jug*)   Who did this?

No answer.

Sanbrooke   Who did this?

Eadie   I did.

Ringing starts in **Eadie**'s *ears.*

Sanbrooke   What is it?

Eadie   Caramel.

Sanbrooke   Caramel? Sugar?

Eadie   Yes.

Sanbrooke   Sugar?

Eadie   Yes.

Sanbrooke   How dare you? How dare you serve me that? Sugar is contraband, sugar is illegal.

Eadie   I was told to make it.

Sanbrooke   By who?

Eadie   Aidan, my Head Chef, he asked.

Sanbrooke   And where is he?

Eadie   I don't know.

Mason   She was asked to make that sir.

Eadie   Sir?

Jana   OK, there's obviously been a mistake here.

Sanbrooke   Kelly, arrest her.

Mr Kelly *looks at* **Mr Costello**.

Anna *and* **Cora** *move to the other side of the room, clutching each other.*

Mason *steps towards* **Eadie** *and* **Anthony** *can't move.*

Sanbrooke   Kelly. I said arrest her, are you deaf?

Anthony   There's rat poison in the caramel.

Eadie   Anthony. Shut up.

Anthony   We're caught Eadie, that's it. We'll have to confess. I'm so sorry /

Eadie   Anthony. Shut up.

Anthony   I'm sorry, I'm so sorry /

In one fluid movement **Eadie** *takes the hunting knife out of* **Mr Kelly**'s *belt, moves towards* **Anthony** *and slits his throat.*

The ringing stops for **Eadie**.

Anna *faints and* **Cora** *catches her. They both fall to the floor.*

Cora *shuts her eyes.*

Eadie (*to* **Sanbrooke**)   What did you do to my sister?

Mr Costello *moves towards* **Eadie** *and* **Mason** *goes to stop him but* **Mr Costello** *grabs a bottle of vodka and smashes him over the head with it.* **Mason** *falls to the floor.*

Eadie (*to* **Sanbrooke**)   What did you do to my sister?

Eadie *picks up the jug of caramel and throws it at* **Sanbrooke**.

Blinded by the sauce, **Sanbrooke** *grabs* **Margot** *who snaps, picks up the shoe and stabs him in the hand with it.*

Margot   Stop fucking touching me.

Sanbrooke *is now pinned to the table.*

Jana *jumps up out of her seat and tries to hold* **Eadie**.

Mr Costello *helps her.*

Jana   It's OK, it's OK.

Mr Kelly *takes the hunting knife off* **Eadie** *and walks around behind* **Sanbrooke** *and slits his throat.*

Margot *begins to have an asthma attack.* **Mr Kelly** *picks up her bag, pulls out her inhaler and takes a long drag out of it before tossing it across the room.*

Mr Kelly *then wipes the handle and throws the knife on the floor.*

Sanbrooke *and* **Anthony** *are bleeding out.*

Mason *is passed out on the floor.*

Jana *and* **Mr Costello** *is holding* **Eadie**.

Cora *is weeping holding* **Anna**.

Stephen *stands shaking when* **Cordelia** *comes back in and screams.*

Mr Kelly *walks over to the camera, which had been recording, and destroys it.*

Fifteen: She Just Snapped

Statements.

Cora   She just. She just snapped.

Anna   I can't remember.

Aidan   She hit me on the head and locked me up.

Jana   I'm sorry, it's a bit of a blur.

Anna   I think I fainted.

Cora   I wasn't looking.

Cordelia   There was blood everywhere. I just saw blood.

Mason   I don't know, she wasn't in her right mind.

Anna (*touching her head*)   I have a bump here.

Cora   I can't believe it.

Mr Costello   This won't be a popular opinion /

Mr Kelly   As I was tending to the first victim /

Mr Costello   With the recent news of her poor sister /

Mr Kelly   The assailant slit the President's throat /

Mr Costello   And the pressure of work, with our visit /

Mr Kelly   I immediately went to subdue /

Mr Costello   I think the girl, grief stricken, lost her mind.

Mr Kelly   And in the struggle, she knocked the camera.

Cordelia   I called the police and spoke to the press.

Jana   I think I fainted when she went for him.

Mason   She's such a good person but she's not well.

Cora   She always liked him.

Anna   They were friends, I think.

Aidan   Anthony was a gentle guy, nervous.

Jana   When I woke up, the President was dead.

Mr Costello   She snapped.

Mr Kelly   She snapped.

Cordelia   She snapped.

Stephen   She must have snapped.

Mason   She's such a good person, please believe me.

Aidan   She put rat poison in the caramel.

Cora   And she slit his throat.

Anna   Everything went black.

Aidan   She was heartbroken.

Mr Costello   She was in anguish.

Mr Kelly   Overcome with loss.

Cordelia   Inconsolable.

Jana   The mental health service in this country /

Stephen   Did I see her kill them?

Jana   Really needs to improve or else this will /

Stephen   Yes. Yes. I did.

Jana   Just keep happening. Again and again and again.

Fifteen: Career Making

Jana *and* **Oisín** *are standing in* **Mr Costello**'s *office three months before the dinner.*

Oisín   Not that I'm not flattered but can we make this quick? I have a regatta gala to attend this evening.

Jana   Of course you do.

Oisín   I must say, I was surprised to hear from you.

Jana   Well I think you're very intelligent Oisín. And right now I need someone intelligent.

Oisín   No one in the party matching up?

Jana   I have a problem that needs to be handled delicately.

Oisín   And what problem is that?

Jana   Off the record.

Oisín   Fine.

Jana   Sanbrooke Martin is ill-equipped for the presidency.

Oisín (*intrigued*)   Really? Says who?

Jana   Don't you agree?

Oisín   Does it matter if I agree?

Jana   He's not fit for the job and I think you are acutely aware of his shortcomings.

Oisín   Ms Kaminski, I'm not about to bad-mouth the President. If you want him gone, just say it.

Jana   I can't do that.

Oisín   Why not?

Jana   He still has the support of the majority in the party. They're stuck on his soaring popularity, the landslide victories. They're not on the ground, talking to the public. They don't understand the hunger and the pain this man has caused. I mean they can read polls, they understand statistics but are stuck in a memory of glory.

Oisín   And they don't support you?

Jana   The National Alliance Party is not quite ready to choose a woman. But they will support me if I am thrust upon them.

Oisín   So how do you do that?

Jana   With your help.

Oisín   I'm not sure I'm interested in helping.

Jana   I'm not asking you to do anything unethical, I'm just asking you to listen. I'm going to put you in touch with a senior advisor, who will give you information about Sanbrooke Martin as and when it happens.

Oisín   What kind of information?

Jana   Evidence of misuse of funds, the disappearance of Junk Advocates, compromising photos of him consuming illegal foods, a love child, if you like.

Oisín   If I like?

Jana   All you need to know is the source is reliable.

Oisín   Have Junk Advocates been disappearing?

Jana   Not yet.

Beat.

Oisín   I have to ask, are you . . . intending on causing anyone harm?

Jana   I'm intending on protecting the Irish people by any means necessary.

Oisín   That didn't answer my question.

Jana   I will cause far less harm than he has.

Oisín   So you want me to carry out a smear campaign against the President in aid of that protection? A bold move but potentially a weak plan. Endgame?

Jana   That disgraced he will have to prematurely resign.

Oisín   And you will step up?

Jana   Something like that.

Oisín   And what would I get out of it?

Jana   Information is what you get out of it. The stories.

Oisín   I'm taking considerable risk here, putting myself out there, for information I need to back up. If anything were to come back on me / I could lose my job.

Jana   It won't. You won't.

Oisín   I need assurances.

Jana   What do you want?

Oisín   Whatever you're willing to give.

Jana   Anything.

Oisín   Just like that?

Jana   Yes.

Oisín   Well then President Kaminski, you have yourself a deal.

Jana   Let's not talk our luck away.

Oisín   I have a feeling luck won't come into this.

Sixteen: Herald

A news report.

CUT TO: A major channel news report. **Oisín** *is in the studio.*

Oisín   Good evening. Today marks one week since The Royal Marine Massacre, an event where three people, including President Sanbrooke Martin, lost their lives. After a rigorous investigation Eadie Birch has been charged with murdering President Martin, her co-worker Anthony Glover and actor Margot Murphy. Birch is the sister of Junk Advocate Lila Birch, whose body was found just days prior to the event.

This afternoon at a press conference, President Jana Kaminski unveiled some shocking findings.

CUT TO: A press conference will a red-eyed **Jana Kaminski**.

Jana   Last week we lost our leader, Sanbrooke Martin, President of the Republic. It is with a heavy heart I say that in the past week evidence has come to light that Sanbrooke Martin was directly involved in the disappearance and murder of nine Junk Advocates, including Lila Birch. Further investigation is needed and we ask the press to be respectful of the families of the deceased. But for now I say I will not rest until the truth is found.

CUT BACK TO: A major channel news report.

Oisín   President Kaminski went on to call a referendum on the Health and Wellness Act which she said 'may have damaged the country beyond repair'.

The President has also nominated former Chief of Staff Ty Costello as her Vice President. More on that later.

A shot of President **Jana Kaminski**, *Vice President* **Ty Costello** *and newly appointed Chief of Staff* **Malachi Kelly**.

Eadie's *eyes.*

A homemade video of **Lila** *flipping pancakes at home. Same clip we saw earlier but the other woman's face is unblurred. It's* **Eadie**, *they're laughing.*

Lila   Why am I flipping these when you're / the

Eadie   I like to see you fail.

Lila   What?

Eadie   I like to see you fail, Lila. Show the people how you fail.

Lila   You have a total of one talent and you lord it over me.

Eadie   My talent is sustenance, food, I am a golden god.

Lila   You've had one mimosa this morning.

Eadie   Mimosa or not I am a golden god.

Lila   Eadie will you help me please? They're sticking.

Eadie   If you weren't so pretty I'd fire you.

Lila   Have you maple syrup?

Eadie   Of course.

Lila   Not for long.

Eadie   Oh they can do one, I'm not going to stop eating sugar.

Lila   So bold.

Eadie   Flip that one now.

Lila *flips the pancake with the pan and whatever way it lands, they are both delighted.*

Eadie*'s eyes welling up.*

We see **Eadie** *from behind, dressed in a white robe, sitting in an all-white room.*

Blackout.

The End.